# Animals Thriving in the Concrete Jungle: A Fascinating Look at Urban Wildlife

As cities continue to expand and encroach upon natural habitats, the relationship between humans and wildlife is evolving.

Contrary to popular belief, cities are not just human-dominated landscapes; they also provide unique opportunities for various animal species to adapt and thrive.

These urban ecosystems have become an unexpected refuge for several species, fostering adaptations that allow them to flourish amidst the hustle and bustle of city life.

From the tiniest insects to larger mammals, let's explore the incredible diversity of animals that have embraced the challenges and opportunities of living in the concrete jungle.

# Pigeons (Columba livia)

Perhaps one of the most iconic urban-dwelling creatures is the pigeon. With their distinctive cooing and ability to navigate dense cityscapes, pigeons have successfully adapted to urban living. They are highly adaptable birds that have made their homes on window sills, rooftops, and bridges. Although often considered a nuisance, pigeons play a significant role in urban ecosystems, aiding in seed dispersal and acting as a food source for predators such as raptors and foxes.

# Raccoons (Procyon lotor)

Raccoons, renowned for their intelligence and dexterity, have capitalized on the abundance of food and shelter in urban areas. These nocturnal bandits have learned to scavenge from garbage bins and compost heaps, making use of the human-generated waste.

They are skilled at urban survival and have adapted to navigate through complex environments, using their inquisitive nature to their advantage.

# Squirrels (Sciurus spp.)

Squirrels are common sights in urban parks and gardens, dashing along power lines and leaping between trees. These agile creatures have mastered the art of thriving in the concrete jungle by finding food in urban green spaces and creating nests in tree hollows and attics.

Their adaptability has even led to behavioral changes, with urban squirrels often becoming less fearful of humans compared to their rural counterparts.

# Foxes (Vulpes vulpes)

In recent years, urban foxes have become a familiar sight in many cities. Escaping the pressure of natural habitats, these cunning creatures have found urban environments to be abundant in food sources and relatively free from predators.

They are known for their adaptability and have learned to coexist with humans, navigating neighborhoods and parks in search of sustenance.

# Rats (Rattus spp.)

While not the most welcome inhabitants of the city, rats have been successful in exploiting human settlements.

Their scavenging behavior allows them to feed on discarded food, and they have adapted to inhabit the nooks and crannies of urban infrastructure.

As a result, rat populations have surged in cities, posing challenges for sanitation and public health.

# Peregrine Falcons (Falco peregrinus)

In a remarkable conservation success story, peregrine falcons have embraced urban living, nesting on skyscrapers and bridges in major cities worldwide.

Once endangered due to pesticides and habitat loss, these birds of prey have found refuge in urban environments, preying on pigeons and other small birds that thrive in cities.

# Monarch Butterflies (Danaus plexippus)

Monarch butterflies, known for their long-distance migrations, have been spotted in urban areas as they traverse across vast landscapes.

While cities may not offer ideal breeding grounds, urban green spaces serve as important refueling stations for these insects during their arduous journeys.

The coexistence of humans and animals in the city is a complex and dynamic relationship. As cities continue to grow, understanding and appreciating the diversity of wildlife that thrives in urban environments become crucial.

By recognizing the adaptations and behaviors of these animals, we can foster more harmonious interactions between humans and the thriving wildlife in our concrete jungles.

Balancing urban development with the preservation of green spaces and wildlife habitats will be vital to ensure that these unique urban ecosystems continue to support the rich biodiversity of animal life within our cities.

We will provide additional space for notes and visualations in the next few pages: